Minimalist

The Best Ways to Simplify your Work Life

© **Copyright 2017 – Ris Jackson All rights reserved.**

This document is geared towards providing exact and reliable information in regards to the topic and issue covered. The publication is sold with the idea that the publisher is not required to render accounting, officially permitted, or otherwise, qualified services. If advice is necessary, legal or professional, a practiced individual in the profession should be ordered.

- From a Declaration of Principles which was accepted and approved equally by a Committee of the American Bar Association and a Committee of Publishers and Associations.

In no way is it legal to reproduce, duplicate, or transmit any part of this document in either electronic means or in printed format. Recording of this publication is strictly prohibited and any storage of this document is not allowed unless with written permission from the publisher. All rights reserved.

The information provided herein is stated to be truthful and consistent, in that any liability, in terms of inattention or otherwise, by any usage or abuse of any policies, processes, or directions contained within is the solitary and utter responsibility of the recipient reader. Under no circumstances will any legal responsibility or blame be held against the publisher for any reparation, damages, or monetary loss due to the information herein, either directly or indirectly.

Respective authors own all copyrights not held by the publisher.

The information herein is offered for informational purposes solely, and is universal as so. The presentation of the information is without contract or any type of guarantee assurance.

The trademarks that are used are without any consent, and the publication of the trademark is without permission or backing by the trademark owner. All trademarks and brands within this book are for clarifying purposes only and are the owned by the owners themselves, not affiliated with this document.

Table of Contents

Introduction iv
Chapter 1 – Know what's essential 6
Chapter 2 – Simplifying your commitments 9
Chapter 3 – Weekly schedules and reviews 13
Chapter 4 – No more meetings.. 16
Chapter 5 – Time 18
Chapter 6 – Your workspace 22
Chapter 7 – Distractions 25
Chapter 8 – Saying no 29
Chapter 9 – All the small things 31
Chapter 10 - It's better to not be perfect 34
Chapter 11 – Delegation 37
Chapter 12 – Body posture 41

Introduction

Did you ever just get into work and start to wonder where the same, stale, old, boring routine came from? Where the monotonous drag of rushed tasks and the never endlessness of pulling your own hair out? I've been there and experienced that too and I can tell you it pushed me to a point where I was down and out.

I had no idea where to go with it all. Never ending streams of paper and work coming out from everywhere that would rush me through my work day for five days a week and I wouldn't have a clue where to start. Something had to be done, and it was at that time I decided that it could go on no longer.

I took it upon myself to go through and find every trick and tip I could that would make my working days that much easier and through the course of this book and the chapters within, I want to share with you what it is that I have found has worked for me and can help you to achieve your goals within your own working life.

I will be showing you how you should value your time and how doing less can alternatively result in gaining more, how creating a basic and simple daily routine can project you further forward than you have ever imagined. People have tried to make this subject something boring, dull and downright dreadful, that is why I have written this book so that you can take all of those long lectures and whiteboard presentations, throw them into the trash and get refreshed. Basic, simple, easy to follow along steps that can help you succeed and ultimately feel better when it's time to go home at the end of the day.

I heard a friend of mine complaining one day that all they ever do is seem to work, put in countless hours of overtime to meet deadlines and finish projects, how they never got to see much of their family and when they could all they could do was think about work. I told him them that I had written a book about this and how to Simplify his work life and offered him a copy to read.

After a week had passed I received a phone call from him telling me how much this book had helped and by implementing just a few of these steps in just a week, had resulted in massive success.

So, I hope that as you read through and come to the end of this book you find just as much value from it as others have and you can start to take control of your own work life right away!

Chapter 1 – Know what's essential

Okay, so starting your day with a mountain of tasks and jobs to do can seem daunting when you start your day. Your mind all cluttered with no idea where to start. How about if you could erase that feeling forever with a few simple steps, how much would that help you?

Not knowing what is essential in the day to day life within your working profession can lead to several difficulties. Confusion, being unorganized and going back and forth. This is no good for anybody.

So, stop what you are thinking about, forget about last week's reports or yesterday's paperwork and clear your mind. I want you to think of and focus on one task that you want to complete today, just one. But it must be essential. Got it? Great.

Focusing

Focus on what you think will be the most important thing for you to get done today. Write it down on a piece of paper and stick it to your computer or make it the background image on your phone so you can see it every time you look at it if you must.

Knowing what's essential is a key part to how you approach your day or even your week. At the start of your day/week you should be highlighting the main task which is going to give you the greatest reward. Once you have done identified it you should focus your entire energy on completing it, forgetting about all the smaller nuisances that throw themselves at you that day as they can wait and can probably be solved in a matter of minutes rather than a couple of hours or more which your essential tasks are going to take and require your full attention.

Keep in mind

Remember this is what you are going to be working towards to complete before the day has ended and never and I repeat, NEVER get into the habit of carrying this over into the next day.

Here's what I want you to do, get a piece of paper, or post it notes for example and write down up to 3 of the most important tasks that you want to complete before the day is over. It could be something as simple as;

File all paperwork

Print all invoices and send them

Create rota for shifts

Now all you must do is simply tick them off as you go along. Devote the first half of your day up until midday towards what you have wrote down, and the physical image of it being there with a tick next to it will see you complete them faster and faster as time goes on as it gives you a sense of accomplishment and especially from doing so in a shorter time than you were previously used to.

Don't lie to yourself

What I see a lot of people doing is creating unrealistic tasks to be completed in a single day. For example, if you have a presentation to complete and need to confer with other colleagues about ideas and inputs, realistically you are not going to get this done as the other people are either going to be out of the workplace or will have other commitments. This means that your main daily task should be unique to yourself and yourself only.

The benefits of being able to identify and execute your day to day tasks will see you completing more and more as each week goes by. And instead of being known as that somebody who takes forever to get things done, you will be seen as somebody who knows what they are doing more than they already do and people will start to come to you for advice and help. Projecting yourself higher so that others can see you as an example.

Chapter 2 – Simplifying your commitments

A problem that many of us have is wanting to do what we really want but with everything that goes on in our lives, trying to find the time seems to work on them seems impossible as we often take on much more than we can handle.

It is going to be likely that you over commit yourself and by saying this I mean that you have too many things going on in your life at the same time which takes up the valuable time that you could be using to complete the important projects that you need to complete. By filling your day with these unnecessary commitments, you are exhausting yourself meaning the energy you could be spending on being more productive is being spent on activities that could wait a day extra or are everyday common things which would not mind being made to wait while you take control of the work you need to produce.

As much as you would like to think you can't do these at the same time. There is only 24 hours in a day and you can only do so much. Be honest with people and tell them that you cannot commit to whatever it was that you had planned that day and you have a high number of important and urgent projects that need completing as soon as possible. This is you putting your productivity first over procrastination.

Slowly but surely you will whittle these down to a select few and notice how much more time you have gained as well as the stress relief on yourself as you have noticed completing your work projects and tasks in this time which in turn makes you feel more productive and accomplished.

Positive commitments

Not all commitments are negative, you don't have to eliminate them to gain positive ground. Instead, making more commitments can be productive if they are the right ones.

Some of the commitments you can make today to better yourself tomorrow could be things such as;

Committing to learning a new skill once a week

Setting yourself a goal of learning just one new skill per week can greatly increase productivity within your job/business. Just think about how much money or time that you spend on other people doing a job for you that if you learned how to do it yourself.

By learning how to do these tasks you not only save yourself money by paying somebody else how to do it, but you also gain a greater understanding about the whole process, how it works and later you can explain how to do it to somebody else so that they too can progress forwards.

I never knew how to do a lot of the smaller things where I used to work and by spending no less than 20 minutes sometimes, I could learn a new skill that benefitted me and saved me time in the future when I needed something done I could do myself in a shorter time than waiting for someone to do it for me. Time is key and you do not want to be wasting it.

Committing to challenging others

If you are in the position to be able to inspire and get the best out of other co-workers, then I highly recommend it. Set daily or weekly goals for those who work around you to help drive them and keep them on track.

More too often do we see people getting lazy and sitting in the same stale position for years on end. Challenging them means that you are consistently trying and hopefully succeeding in bringing out the best from within. Given no opportunity to do this means that those around you are not moving forward and not gaining the confidence that they need about their job roles, and in the long run this comes back and reflects on you.

The more energy and opportunities you give for others to show you how they can work and show what they are made of will likely mean the more that they will use that energy to help you by working more efficiently.

Committing to working with others

Working alone can become a routine where you walk in, sit down, open the computer or laptop and proceed to crawl through that day's work/project. Being along can mean that you only have the one brain to count on and as they say, two brains are better than one.

Making a schedule to meet regularly with somebody who shares the same interests or works in the same area as yourself means that you can share ideas and get another person's perspective on the task at hand. They may point out flaws in your work that you would never have seen otherwise or guide you in the right direction if you do not know where to start. Meeting for a couple of hours a week with somebody else can greatly improve your productivity and should not be forgotten.

Getting used to committing yourself to positive events and situations will get you into the habit of bettering your future self. Leaving the old, time wasting commitments behind that could wait for another time will see you learn more and you will thank yourself for it later on in life.

Remember the basic steps

- Say no to the things that can wait
- Only commit to positive outcomes
- If it's going to make you go out of your way, forget about it

Chapter 3 – Weekly schedules and reviews

Being able to review your set of tasks and to-do lists can be something you can dedicate a short 10 minutes at the end of every week to do. Eliminate all the tasks you created that week (you should be deleting them all as you have been super productive) and creating new ones ready for the week ahead is something that does not take very long to do.

Set up an event for each day on your calendar with the tasks you want to complete for that day/week, that way you are reminded every time you log in to your computer or your smart phone or you could even set an alarm to go off at certain times so that in a way it becomes annoying until you complete the task in return making it a more successful day.

Little things like this can help you stay on track. You don't need a big list either, just select the important things for that day and write them down. I find It's a great way of storing things to do as sometimes I forget what it is that needs completing and by the end of the week when somebody reminds me of what I should have done 3 days ago, it is already too late.

You may be wondering what value this practice holds which is totally understandable. Here are just a few ways in which it has helped me along the way.

The past week

How likely is it that you check back on the previous week's work and tasks that you had set yourself? Doing this can urge you to review any meetings or projects which may remind you to send that all important email or look over notes taken that you would otherwise forget about had you not reviewed all of this.

The future

Learning to review your upcoming week is a good way to stop any sudden surprises like last minute meetings or work that may need to be handed in. Looking over your schedule will remind you to prepare anything needed for specific days and help you to start working on any logistics such as getting from one place to another to make it in time.

Mondays

Everybody hates Monday mornings, the first day back at work after a great weekend. Coffee cups in hand and the zombie like walk into work. Nobody is motivated and holds a negative mindset as they do not want to be there.

By holding your weekly reviews at the start of the week you have not yet reached full speed and give yourself the opportunity to plan properly and go over things without having any other midweek distractions. Once this becomes a habit, everything will fall into place as it gives you control and can provide you with some risk management benefits such as not running the risk of missing those important deadlines or follow up appointments that otherwise without the planning within the weekly review, you may have forgotten about.

Benefits

I find that the benefits of having these reviews is that they can be used to get clear, current and creative. Clear all your workspace and figure out what is important and what is not, delete all of your old emails, more importantly empty your head. Out with old and in with the new. Being current means that you should take into consideration what is happening now. Get that done first before making other plans. Creative, start thinking about the things you want to do, create space for the little things you can squeeze in that you really want to get done, not what others want or need you to do.

Chapter 4 – No more meetings

Meetings have become that word that nobody at work wants to hear. The hours spent sitting down, moving around trying to get comfy after becoming numb both in your body and in your mind. Its just a way for the big wigs to feel important. Nobody should have to be subdued to this kind of torture.

I know what it feels like

A short story about why I think this is something that I found to be one of the most pointless and most time-consuming things that can be used in the work place and should be eradicated completely.

From personal experience, I remember working at a certain company and being made to travel to another city which would take up to 2 hours to get to. This was something that happened once at the beginning of every month to discuss what our goals were and how we were going to achiever them within our cities store.

So, wake up early, get ready, super tired, overpriced coffee in the train station, a rush out of the train at the other side, up the stairs and sit there for a further 5 hours being told pointless and boring information that could have been sent and communicated by other means. A waste of my time and day that could have been better spent.

It's amazing what a click can do

Yes, that's right. All this information can be sent at the click of a button and with the numerous amounts of social media, social chat applications such as WhatsApp and Facebook, it dawned on me at how stuck in the old times that a lot of companies are.

Because of this I was made to spend half of my day on a rabbit hunt for information which would be more efficiently discussed over a message sent from your computer and without making people travel from all over the country. And if your place of work does hold regular meetings, try to get them to commit to holding conference calls instead.

At the end of the day it is your time which you should be valuing and how to spend it in the most efficient ways possible. The next time your boss asks you to attend a meeting tell them you can't make it and to email you the discussions or questions that they may have.

Overtime you will notice how much of a difference it makes not spending time in a board room and wasting your whole day travelling. Instead you are spending time being productive and completing work that really matters.

Implement

Having yourself or whoever it is you may work for become open to the idea of social media can make all of this faster and more efficient for everybody. If companies installed software so that they could be linked across all branches, whether it be an internal system or a secret group online where only work colleagues could use it. With a basic internet connection, all of this could be made simpler. And at the end of the day, that's what all of this is about.

Chapter 5 – Time

Time is just one of those things that you are never going to get back no matter what you do. Learning how to use it efficiently and wisely will benefit you massively in the long run if you start now.

One of the things I have noticed is that if I know I have all day to do something then there is no real deadline, no point as to which something must be completed as such. If I know I have eight hours to complete something that is only going to take me an hour at the most to finish, then often I was filling the time in between with useless procrastination like scrolling down through social media posts that I had already seen a thousand times or looking at clothing sites daydreaming about what it was that I wanted to buy next.

It wasn't until the last hour of the day which I had left myself to try and speed through and complete that days job that I was flustered and running around crazily trying to get it done. It wasn't a nice feeling having to be like this all the time and I would have saved myself a lot of hassle if I had just managed my time a little bit better.

Deadlines

Your work will always seem to expand and fill your time that is available if you allow it to. If you allow yourself to work all night or all day for example, then you will start to notice you will always have a lot of work to do as you are giving that opportunity for more work to be created before you have set yourself a deadline to finish what you haven't even started yet.

What I started to do was to install a program onto my computer that I was using and every time I would go to my favourite site that I would often waste time on each day, it would only allow me a maximum of 10 minutes per day on that specific site. Doing something like this will benefit you so much and you will start to notice massive results in the first week.

Giving yourself a maximum of one hour to complete a certain job works well too as you are forcing yourself to work faster and more efficiently in a shorter space of time. This way you can start to power through at least three times the work you could do before when you were stuck procrastinating unable to pull yourself away.

Taking breaks

Taking breaks whilst working is very important, working too long and too hard can see the quality of your work decrease rapidly as this is due to you losing concentration, becoming tired, hungry and continuous eye strain if you sit at a computer for most of the day. You need to take control of how you break up your working hours, as working for too long can lead to all the previous reasons.

One of the places that I used to work at not so long ago had a clause in the contract that everybody who worked there had to take a twenty-minute break every one and a half hours due to the levels of concentration needed. This way everybody was fresh and could continue at a high standard throughout the day as the amounts of time to replenish yourself to keep on going was regular.

If you work from home or for yourself for example, trying to give yourself regular breaks is a hard thing to do as all you want to do is work throughout the day to complete whatever it is that you are doing. Your home becomes your office and dragging yourself away from work is a little harder than if you are forced to take breaks by a boss or somebody telling you what to do.

Try setting regular alarms every ninety minutes for breaks and another one fifteen minutes after that one to indicate when it is time to get back to work. At first it will be hard to get used to but over time this will become a regular ordeal that will point you in the right direction.

By doing all of this, it makes the time that you spend working that much more valuable as you are at your best, and during that time you are producing your best work. It's what everybody wants from you and is more productive.

Quick tips

There are many ways to manage your time throughout the day and it should be something that you make a priority, it's the one thing we can't get back from our day so you should learn how to use and manage it wisely. Below are some ways as to how you can do this.

Take atleast 30 minutes at the start of your day to plan what's going to happen with the rest of it and don't start any work until you have planned out what you want to do with your day. It doesn't have to be complicated, basic bullet point ideas will be fine.

Before you make any phone calls, spend a couple of minute thinking about what you want to say and some answers to questions you think that you may get. This will cut down any unnecessary time wasting while on the phone thinking about what it is you wanted to say in the first place. It also makes you look more professional as a quick, precise, on the spot thinker and deliverer.

Don't allow the unimportant details stop you from moving forward. I have been a victim of this as I used to constantly want everything to be perfect and to include every detail that I could find. After learning to forget about this and just to get the bulk of the work I needed doing done, I was able to get more out of my day and did not waste time doing work that did not need doing in the first place.

Give yourself some free time in-between tasks, your mind and body need it and you cant power through the day all in one go, finding yourself rushing from one task to the next. Giving yourself this time will allow your brain to relax and you to refresh yourself ready to take on the next piece of work without your mind being clogged up.

If you find yourself waiting around for reasons such as Doctors appointments, waiting in a line or if you are travelling, this can be a great opportunity to read an article that you have been meaning to finish or continue listening to a podcast that can give you information and knowledge on something you are interested in. People are always saying that they don't have time to do these things, but part of it is finding the time within other things you are doing.

These tips are just some of the ways that you can use your time throughout the day to greatly improve your work life. Simple yet effective.

Chapter 6 – Your workspace

This is going to be the main area where you are spending much of your day. Whether it is a desk, a van, a car or an airport lounge over in the other side of the world. Your workspace for the day is something that you should value and look after as it sets the tone on how you approach it and the attitude that you take.

For example, you go into work one morning and everything is a mess, papers lying across the desk unorganized and piled up to the ceiling, trash everywhere, mail unopened that has been forgotten about and which you never want to even start to look at because of the dreaded endlessness of it all. This would instantly put you in a negative mindset and a bad mood which is something that you do not want.

Whereas if you were to start your day knowing where everything was that you needed for the day. Desktop tidy, paperwork and files all in the correct places, no stacked-up piles of notes. All of this means that you are not wasting time going through the mountain of work that would usually be in the way, meaning you can work faster and smarter throughout.

I myself was not a very tidy person, I was a mirror image of the first example. But even by changing things a little at a time it meant that now I can be a smarter and faster individual whenever I have work to complete.

Start today, even if it is just one area. Spending 15 minutes in the morning to sort out and file your paperwork or clear your emails for example, can make a whole world of difference. And once that initial 15 minutes has been spent to organise these specific areas within your working area you will never have to go back and do it again.

You might not notice it now but it is these small implications that can lead you onto the right path to success and being that productive person you have always wanted to be.

Your workspace and its environment has a huge effect on your state of mind and productivity. A rule of thumb that I tend to go by is this; If it does not help me to do my job more effectively then put it away.

Connect your technology

By interconnecting all your technology, it makes your daily work life a lot easier. By having everything linked together whether it be laptops, desktops, projectors, printers and scanners, it can make the day run smoothly and seamlessly transition one thing to another instead of wasting time connecting multiple devices to others with applications and programs that do not work. By standardizing all the equipment and how it runs, everybody can utilize everything efficiently.

Little things can make a big difference

It does not have to be much, maybe having a few plants here and there, snacks and drinks in the break room or a games room for colleagues to interact with each other. Things like this will help to keep moral high in the workplace and having staff happy means that they will feel better about themselves and perform better.

Hiring

If you are a person who just hates to clean and tidy, then you might want to think about hiring a cleaner. None of the work with all of the benefits. You get to come to your workspace everyday knowing that everything is in order and nothing will need to be sorted out. A tidy area so that you can get straight down to work.

Assign discard dates

You don't need to keep every piece of paper, cardboard, envelope, package and who knows whatever else it is that you get on a day to day basis, but you should not be letting yourself horde everything in drawers until they are bursting at the edges. Some documents that you may get such as financial documents and legal pieces need to be kept for a certain amount of time understandably, but a notice about a package being delivered or the latest pizza offers from the local takeaway can be thrown away. Give yourself a short space of time to keep things like invoices etc and them throw them away, they aren't needed anymore and are just taking up valuable desk space.

Clear everything

Take everything off your desk or workspace. Leave it completely blank. Now go through each item that you have just removed and ask yourself if you really do need it, you will find you have less at the end than what you began with before you cleared it all. The reason being that over time we get into the habit of collecting useless items, mountains of pens which half of them don't work anyway and just become professional hoarders. Throw away what you don't need and only keep what is essential.

Chapter 7 – Distractions

Now I want you to think about something. How many times have you been in the middle of a dinner or a really interested conversation and you hear that ringing and the buzzing coming from your mobile, or that 'ping' noise you get when an email comes through leading you to stray and distract you from what you were doing in the first place. Annoying, right?

So, why would you want to have the same thing happen to you whilst you are supposed to be productive and focusing on important work. Giving yourself the opportunity to be distracted by things that can wait an extra hour or two can only lead to destruction to yourself.

Make yourself unreachable

That's right, if you can, remove yourself from others around you entirely. One of the main causes for distraction is other people so you need to remove yourself as far away as possible.

The best way to get work done is when you are not being interrupted. Even though the people you work with or work around could very well be the nicest people on the planet, listening to them talk about what they did on the weekend, what their vacation plans are going to be and where they are going, the gossip that surround their work day.

These are the types of things that you do not want to be getting caught up in. What you should be doing is removing yourself from the scene of the crime and try to find a quiet and secluded area, whether this is a Library, a separate room or even if you must book a room somewhere in an office space just so you can work undisturbed. If you can't remove yourself from the environment, then you need to try and learn how to control it.

This could be the simple thing of putting in ear plugs to drown the noise out, or simply asking your fellow workers or people around you to keep their voices down and tell them that you are working on a very important task.

Turn it off!

Now that there are so many different technological devices being invented and made, the list of digital distractions is never ending. If working from home, you will find that this is one of the majors in distractions. It's just too easy to turn the TV on catch that latest episode of your favourite series, or carry on watching the movie you got half way through the night before.

Having your cell phone next to you is another major bad point, its just to easy to be checking Facebook or Instagram to see those latest posts by friends or carrying on a conversation that can wait until the end of the day. Telling yourself that you will only watch 10 minutes or just talk for 5, all seems to roll ever so quickly into several hours wasted doing so and before you know it you have lost all will power to concentrate on what you were supposed to be doing.

The best thing you can do is set yourself strict time to which you can use these devices and not use them until your work for the day has been done. If you feel strongly and you are dedicated to your work, you will see an increase in speed within your work.

Nobody's home

Another big distraction can be your co-workers and having them stop by your office throughout the day. This is something that I have had on numerous occasions, one minute you are sat there working at a steady pace and suddenly one of your co-workers happens to walk by and knock on your door.

Before you know it a simple hello has turned into an hour long chat about anything and everything, then as you look at the clock on the wall and hour has seemed to pass without you even knowing it. Have this happen a couple of times each day and that is valuable time that you are losing to a distraction that could wait. Something that I implemented was to have a sign on the front of my door with times that I could be reached at.

This meant that people understood that no matter how much they tried I was not available until the time slots as advertised on my office door. Doing this meant that not only did I get more work done by eliminated this all together, but others around me did too as they were gaining the extra time that they would have spent in my office talking to me, on working towards their own tasks for that given day.

Clean up

You may not think so but having a messy workspace can become a distraction. Lots of different things around you such as notes, letters, photos and food are all things that can catch your eye and lead you to stray away from what is important and what you should be doing. By cleaning everything up around you, you are no longer tempted to find other things to do.

Rewarding yourself

Something that works for me is telling myself that after I have done a certain task I will go and get something to eat, make myself a coffee or treat myself to some chocolate. Little things like this can help to spur you on if you lack the motivation. Giving yourself smaller rewards for having achieved what it was you should be doing anyway can become very useful and over time you should notice that you don't even need to do this anymore as you have forced yourself to get into a habit.

If you are one of the lucky ones

If you are fortunate enough to be able to work from home, then try to create and enforce set hours to which you work within. You may not have to wake up every morning and travel to work but you still need to create some sort of routine, not only for yourself but for others around you also. Your family and friends should know what time you are going to be busy and when not to disturb you. Less distractions. More tasks and work completed. Everybody is happy.

Chapter 8 – Saying no

Don't you just wish that you could plant your feet firmly on the ground and say no sometimes? A lot of us feel the need to agree with people or go the extra mile for others because we are afraid of letting them down, seeming to not care, being criticized or having others think you are selfish. But once you learn to be able to say this magic word it can earn you a lot of respect from not just the people you work with but also those closest to you, including yourself.

Not being able to say no to others requests and demands can leave you feeling exhausted, worn out and tired. You may find that because you have commitments you agreed to o agreeing to help other people, now you don't have enough time to do your own work, which in turn takes you nowhere.

Don't wait until you are flat out on the bed, tired and worrying about the things you shouldn't even have on your mind that day on top of everything else. Take a step back from it all now and learn a few steps that can guide you towards saying no to others and freeing up some time for yourself.

Keep your response a simple one

It goes without saying that firm and to the point is the key here. A simple "No thanks, but maybe another time" or even "I can't today, sorry". This should be all you are saying in your response as you don't need to over apologise for something you are not obliged to say yes to in the first place.

Don't feel guilty for saying no

It is important for people to hear the word no from time to time as if not everybody would expect to get what they want all the time, which isn't good for anybody. If a co-worker knew that every time they wanted something doing and they could just come to you and ask you to do it for them because they know for a fact you will say yes, this does not help either person. You are losing your valuable time, and the other is never going to learn any valuable skills to be productive. Be the person in charge and set some boundaries in the workplace by saying no.

Explain why

Giving an answer such as this one can be a hard pill to swallow for the person hearing it, so explaining to them the reason 'why' you are saying no to their request can make it easier for others to understand your reasoning and also maybe affect what they ask of you in the future.

Never look back

What I mean by this is that you should not be changing your mind. Once you have said no that means it is final. Once you get in to the habit of changing your mind you will find yourself moving backwards rather than forwards and going back and forth, others will see that you are weak in your decision making and will see opportunity to change your mind by being the persistent one. Instead, focus on how good it feels to say no to something you really do not want to do, something that will take your energy away and leave you feeling worse off.

Try to push your feelings of guilt aside, do not feel guilty, you have just as much right for saying no as the other person does for asking you the question in the first place.

Chapter 9 – All the small things

People tend to overlook and forget about all of the smaller details which need taking care of throughout your day to day life. Ignoring them and not taking care of yourself in the simplest of ways can have a huge impact on your performance.

Health and wellbeing is one of the most important elements of a good working day and you should be concerned about how your working environment impacts your general wellbeing. There are several simple ways that you can improve your wellbeing and also your performance and productivity whilst at work.

With half of your waking day being spent working and in and around the work environment it is important that you make sure to look after yourself and how to better your health during this time.

Eating well

A lot of people may be familiar with the canteen style dinners and vending machine snacks provided at a lot of work places. These can often be fatty, sugary foods that give a short and limited boost of energy and then leave you feeling tired and lazy leading you to repeat the process just to stay atop.

Instead, get into the habit of bringing your own food and snacks into work and control what types of food you eat throughout the day. Food is your fuel and the quality of it reflects on how well you perform.

If you don't find the time before you go to work to make yourself a decent meal to take with you then you can always aim to at least take nutritious snacks with you to maintain energy and concentration throughout the day, such as nuts and fruits.

Move around

Look for ways you can add more activity to your day. Getting up for 5 minutes every hour to take a short walk and to stretch your legs can be a great feeling and get you away from the computer screen or whatever work task it is that you are doing. Sitting down for long periods of time can produce negative effects on your body which is not good, especially when working.

Take the longer route around the office to collect something from the printer or making your way to the kitchen to make a drink. The extra time spent away will refresh your body, get the blood flowing again and prepare you for the next session.

Keep yourself hydrated

Everybody knows that your working day may consist of 8, 10 or even 12 hour days and due to whatever your role is, this means that you may require high levels of concentration and in the day these levels may drop.

One of the reasons you may be feeling a drop-in energy and your mood plummeting is down to dehydration making it hard to focus, making it tempting to go and grab a coffee, tea or energy drink to try and help boost these back up.

The trick to breaking this cycle is water. Get into the habit of keeping a bottle of water at your desk or carry one around with you if you are moving around a lot. If you want to, you could switch it for flavoured waters, coconut water or even buy and infuser and fill it with your favourite fruits to keep it fresh instead of having plain water all the time.

Plan

Start to make a plan for each day with certain goals for you to hit. They don't have to be hard or complicated but maybe things like.

- Drinking two bottles of water before lunch time
- Eating every half an hour (snacks such as nuts, raisins, etc)
- Taking a walk around the office or wherever it may be every hour

Keeping to these simple schedules will see you become more alert and awake producing more quality that comes from you in the day.

Chapter 10 - It's better to not be perfect

Being able to leave all your work behind you at the end of your day sounds great, and many of us wish that we could leave when we mean to, go home and not think about it anymore and worry ourselves for the rest of the day. But realistically how often does that happen? How often can you tell yourself that what's done is done and you don't ever need to go back to it.

Some people find it very hard to let things go and because of that end up putting a lot of pressure and stress on themselves to perfect what is already done, creating more work for yourself so that you are constantly feeling busy.

Trying to be a perfectionist can stop you from becoming your best. You become less effective, constantly adding more to what you think will be a positive addition to your work when they are not adding any real value. Filling a document with more information could render it useless as it is full of fluff, or trying to add more images into a design piece could make it look ugly.

Becoming a procrastinator is a label that you may find yourself falling into as you try to wait for that perfect moment to get your task done. This leads you to overcomplicate it as you have spent such a long time waiting and thinking about what it is that you have to do, you never actually get to the end result as the thought of it becomes intimidating as you may not be able to do your best, so keep pushing it further and further away until the time is too late.

More is less

I'm sure everybody is familiar with the phrase "Less is more" and I love that. But in the case of perfecting your work and lowering the extra hours that it brings with it, more can be less, especially if you have multiple projects that you have got to get completed in a certain time frame.

Being able to perfect everything that you do sounds great and in an ideal world everybody would love to be like that. But the hours that you spend trying to perfect one piece of work are being wasted as it means that an already completed task is being prolonged for no reason at all.

What sounds better, one perfected piece that only you yourself would feel content in, or 5 total pieces of work/projects being completed that your boss or other colleagues would find as equally outstanding? It is only yourself holding you back from getting more done.

Instead try to learn to be content with having completed what it is that you are doing and then swiftly moving on to the next. Once you have done an extra one or two tasks you will begin to see that more certainly is less as you are accomplishing more content wise than quality wise and you won't be spending the hours revisiting finished work.

If after you want to go back and edit any work or make any slight adjustments, then be sure to make them quick and minimal. You have all your work completed now, don't be the burden to stop them being done forever.

It doesn't matter

Being able to forget about being number one all the time does have its benefits in the long run and crosses over into other areas of your work and general day to day life. Below are some of the things that can have an effect on you for wanting to be perfect all the time and why it is overrated.

You would become un-relatable to the people you know, there would be no common ground regarding any of the work you do and you may even find yourself looking down on them.

You wouldn't learn anything new within your area of work. One of the benefits of working with others is that there is always an opportunity to learn and find new things out about yourself, if you no longer have that option then as well as no longer being able to extend your knowledge about your work but you would never find anything new about yourself either.

You would not be as resilient as other people and would have no opportunities to build on it. What I mean by this is that when things don't go to plan we have to find ways to overcome, adapt and use what skills we already have to solve the issue and in turn we gain more knowledge and skills to take forward with us to use the next time something like this happens.

Stress levels will drop and your free time will be yours again.

Chapter 11 – Delegation

Whether you are your own boss, are a manager at a company or have a lot of work on your plate in general, it can all become a little too much sometimes and you may find yourself up in the clouds with no idea where to begin and the striking fear that you will never complete what you must do. Thinking you are a superhero and you can do it all yourself but the total weight of it all can metaphorically crush you.

This is where delegation comes in, being able to use other co-workers to help yourself and themselves to achieve the full potential of their and your skillset. You must remember the real meaning of the word though, meaning that you are delegating work to others based on their individual skillsets to help achieve and finish the work that they have been given. Never give impossible mountains of work to people that you just can't physically do yourself as they also can never achieve this and will just continue the vicious cycle and nothing productive will come of it.

What are the benefits of this

Being able to hand off your day to day tasks and work to other co-workers will show that you trust in them and their available skillset to achieve what you can't do just on your own. Giving out responsibility in the form of work shows that you trust in the certain persons/persons and in return can make them hungrier for more and more, should you be able to give it to them another time if they can handle it.

Handing out responsibility in this form is not just a benefit for yourself, it also helps to boost the morale of your colleagues and releasing some of the heavier responsibilities that you once had can help to further your own wellbeing and make your life a lot easier.

The reason that you hired people in the first place is because you saw something in each and every one of them, whether it be a certain skill, personality trait, something positive that they can bring to the team. Never forget this. These people are here to help you, not just stand around and fill a hole. Delegating tasks around the people that surround you will ultimately give you more free time to do what is most important. The time to create. Being able to plan out a business meeting, presentation, piece of design work or write an all-important document. This is time that you should be valuing and creating for yourself by delegating across the work force.

Benefiting your team members

Alright so we know that being able to delegate helps you to achieve more and benefits you, but how can it help those you are delegating to? This is something you should keep in mind, you should be able to help others in certain ways whilst giving them work tasks to do so that it does not look like you are using them as slaves so to speak. Being able to show them that they are gaining from this as well as you are is important.

Development

When delegating to your team members sometimes you need to be able to teach them new skills before they go ahead with what you have given them. This is a great way for you to develop your team, teach them the skills needed that they did not know before to help them achieve these tasks and new goals and make them a more versatile, important part of the workforce.

Self-esteem will grow after handing out work as it shows others that you trust in them to handle it and raises morale. This can always help to motivate your team as they are now learning new things and wanting to produce high quality work to prove to you that they are fit for the job a second time around.

Your own ability

Obviously, everybody does not know how to do everything in the world. That is why you hired the people that you did. Because they know how to do things better or that you do not know how to do at all.

Being able to hand down work for others that are more than capable of completing is the best way to start if you aren't all that confident in your own abilities that are needed to complete work, being able to delegate the whole process is a giant leap towards becoming a better boss and creating a better team that surrounds you.

Staying where you are

The reason a lot of people leave their current jobs is because they are not being given any opportunities to further and better themselves resulting in something they once liked to do turning into a stale, old, boring job that they just want to get out of.

Giving people that opportunity that they are looking for can be a huge factor into how many people actually love their job and want to work for you rather than being that person who only comes to work to do the minimal requirements and leave unhappy at the end of the day.

Give people work that they are going to be proud about and that they can show you how well they can do it is something that you should be doing if you aren't already. Keep those that are valuable close to you and don't give them a reason to want to leave.

Chapter 12 – Body posture

Having to spend a large portion of your day at work whether its sitting down or standing up, over time your body will begin to feel the strain. Therefore good, consistent body posture is important to making this time you spend every day a much easier one.

Being able to sit and stand with the proper body alignment means that you can work much more efficiently without getting tired and your body aching as quick as it may usually do. Taking note of your body posture is one of the first steps to combating old habits and taking away all the strain and pain from your spine, knees, hips and other body parts as well as relieving the stress that came with it.

Studies have also shown that bad posture can be a cause for energy loss, depression and can rapidly lower your energy levels. Mix all of the above with a strenuous job and you have a big problem on your hands. Sitting at a desk for most of your day is not a great way to treat your body, but there are some things that you can do to help prevent bad body posture and the effects it can cause.

Uncross your legs

The proper way to sit in a chair requires you to sit with your feel flat on the floor, not crossing your legs, putting them straight out in front of you or crossed on your seat. This is because if you are sitting down for long periods of time you need the flow of blood to flow freely around your body and this includes those two things underneath the desk!

Support pillows

If you have regular problems with lower back pain and are always moving from side to side just trying to get comfy then use a support pillow, these are usually small foam pillows that are shaped to help guide you into the proper position and help to eradicate your back problems. You could also use a rolled-up jumper or coat if you have one near you.

Slouching

A problem that many of us have been told about sometime in our lives, whether as a child or now, it's easy to slouch when standing about either leaning on something or just to 'take the weight off, but over time it can have a lasting effect on your body if you don't look after it. If you do have a problem with slouching a good way to combat this and get back to standing up straight is to imagine that there is a piece of string attached to the top of your head and it is pulling you upwards. Just by being able to constantly visualize this wherever you are can easily guide you into a sense of proper position and more comfort along the road.

These are just a small sample of things that you can do to help improve your posture. But I do recommend you start these today if you have any kind of pain or implications due to your job. It can make it much more easier on yourself.